D0998769

HIP-HOP hitmakers

THE STORY OF
NO LIMIT RECORDS

Jim Whiting

MC **Mason Crest**
Philadelphia

HIP-HOP hitmakers

Mason Crest
370 Reed Road
Broomall, PA 19008
www.masoncrest.com

Copyright © 2013 by Mason Crest, an imprint of National Highlights, Inc.

Printed and bound in the United States of America.

CPSIA Compliance Information: Batch #HHH040112-10.
For further information, contact Mason Crest at 1-866-MCP-Book

First printing
1 3 5 7 9 8 6 4 2

Library of Congress Cataloging-in-Publication Data

Whiting, Jim, 1943-
  The story of No Limit Records / Jim Whiting.
     p. cm. — (Hip-hop hitmakers)
  Includes bibliographical references and index.
   ISBN 978-1-4222-2118-1 (hc)
   ISBN 978-1-4222-2131-0 (pb)
   ISBN 978-1-4222-9470-3 (ebook)
  1. No Limit Records—Juvenile literature. 2. Sound recording industry—United States—
Juvenile literature. I. Title.
   ML3792.N6W55 2012
   338.7'61782421649--dc23
                                        2011035330

Photo credits: Associated Press: 30; FilmMagic: 45; Getty Images: cover, 27, 35, 38; used under license from Shutterstock, Inc.: 10 (top), 14, 42, 49; Helga Esteb / Shutterstock.com: 8, 53, 54; Featureflash / Shutterstock.com: 4; Adam J. Sablich / Shutterstock.com: 33; Tristan Scholze / Shutterstock.com: 18; Stocklight / Shutterstock.com: 50; Dana Ward / Shutterstock.com: 10 (bottom); U.S. Army Corps of Engineers: 17; Wikimedia Commons: 12.

3 1558 00276 8703

Contents

Rapper and hip-hop entrepreneur Percy "Master P" Miller appears with his son, Romeo. At the 2010 VH1 Hip Hop Honors show, Romeo and other former No Limit artists, including Mystikal and Silkk the Shocker, performed a musical montage of No Limit's biggest hits.

Getting due Recognition

In early June 2010, many of the biggest names in hip-hop gathered in New York City. The occasion was the annual VH1 Hip-Hop Music Awards. Host Craig Robinson, a television and movie actor, oversaw a tribute to hip-hop music from the South. It was the first time a particular region had been singled out for praise at the hip-hop music awards, which began in 2004.

During the show, which aired June 7, 2010, tributes were performed for a number of singers or groups with southern origins. They included Luther "Luke" Campbell, J Prince/Rap-A-Lot, Jermaine Dupri, Timbaland, 2 Live Crew, and Organized Noize. Also honored was Percy "Master P" Miller, who had founded No Limit Records, one of the hottest hip-hop labels in the 1990s.

OVERCOMING PROBLEMS

Master P grew up in the Calliope Projects in New Orleans. When he was young, the city had the reputation of "Murder Capital of the United States." New Orleans has the highest murder rate in the country—ten times the national average. The rate of murder and other violent crime is even higher in the Calliope Projects than in other parts of the city. For Master P, violent crime became very personal. One of his brothers was shot to death. Another was involved in a killing and sentenced to life in prison.

VH1

VH1 stands for Video Highlights 1. It is a cable network that was established in 1985 as a spinoff from MTV. Originally it served as a "softer" alternative that would appeal to older viewers than MTV. In the beginning VH1 featured music videos such as light rock, jazz and R&B. Some notable artists the network carried were singers Elton John and Whitney Houston and trumpet player Kenny G.

In the mid-1990s it expanded its offerings to include edgier music, such as rock and rollers the Red Hot Chili Peppers and rappers such as Eminem. The network also had music-related series such as *Behind the Music*. Each episode profiled an individual musician or group and showed the problems they had to overcome to achieve success.

The network's popularity began to fade in the early 2000s and viewership decreased. As a result, VH1 changed much of its format, with particular emphasis on pop culture and reality-based programming. Some of its most popular offerings included what were called "celebreality," series that followed less-regarded but still well-known stars. It also added awards programs to recognize achievements in hip-hop and other areas.

Today VH1 is one of the most widely watched cable networks. Nearly a million people tune in on prime time every night.

Yet Master P managed to overcome these obstacles and start No Limit Records. In fact, those obstacles might have helped contribute to his success. As he explained to Margena Christian of *Jet* magazine,

"I was in the streets so I was a tough guy and nobody could mess over me. Then, I was well educated. I think it's hard to beat somebody that knows both sides. People come in and try to bull you, but if you've been there before, can't nobody really play you like that."

Master P built No Limit into one of the most important hip-hop labels in the mid-to-late 1990s. The company sold about 75 million albums. Many of the company's albums were certified gold or platinum and featured some of the biggest names in hip-hop. In addition, Master P developed other businesses. These made him one of the wealthiest black *entrepreneurs* in the country.

FAST FACT

In the music industry, the designations *gold* and *platinum* refer to how many copies an album sells. A gold album has sales of at least 500,000 copies, while platinum means sales topping 1 million.

LEAVING A LEGACY

Some people in the VH1 audience may not have been aware of No Limit. Its best years had occurred a decade earlier. That hardly lessened the label's importance or its significance. As Andrew Noz explained in an article about the event:

"Though No Limit wasn't the first Southern label to gain national attention, they proved to be the most influential of the region's breakthrough acts, setting both a business model and an aesthetic for the artists and labels that followed. P brought Louisiana hip-hop to the radio and lined the racks of Sam Goodys everywhere with blindingly blingish Pen N Pixel covers, releasing well over 100 albums during a relatively short reign....the catalog and legacy still stands."

Master P (right) attends a 2011 music industry event with his son Romeo and daughter Cymphonique. During the 1990s, Master P's No Limit Records was one of the most successful hip-hop labels, and helped to make the entrepreneur a multimilionaire.

Master P was justifiably proud of that legacy, especially since he had succeeded without the support of a major **record label.** As he told Shaheem Reid of MTV News, "We accomplished something that nobody did, to be able to sell 75 million records independently and to be honored for hip-hop is a blessing and lets you know we been dong the right thing."

During the evening, some of the biggest names in hip-hop performed the music of the honorees. In Master P's case, one was his brother Silkk the Shocker, who said, "It's very good to finally see [Master P] get honored for it. And then, I think a lot of people out there also appreciate what he's done . . . to actually perform and give back to him and show him what he means to us, that's amazing for me."

Another was Mystikal, who performed one of Master P's signature songs, "Make 'Em Say Uhh." A third was Master P's son Romeo, who performed another major hit, "I'm 'Bout It."

MOVING ON

Romeo's participation in the event was significant for another reason. Master P was passing his musical torch to his sons—especially Romeo, the oldest—after nearly two decades in the business.

Romeo was aware of the significance of the gesture. In a letter he posted to the website ballerstatus.com on the same day as the awards, he said,

> "My dad passed the No Limit torch to me and I'm prepared to continue his legacy and make the next generation better. . . . Most African American athletes and entertainers make money for a few years, but lose it due to lack of education and financial literacy. And I've been groomed to break that cycle. . . . I've seen life through my father's eyes, that's why I'm focused and prepared."

Master P may have retired from hip-hop. He was hardly going to retire from public life. He wanted to use his money to benefit other people.

As the evening drew to a close, Master P may have let his thoughts drift back through the years to his boyhood in New Orleans and how unlikely it was that he had managed to find himself in front of a national television audience.

New Orleans (top) is one of the most popular tourist destinations in the United States. Visitors spend up to five billion dollars in the "Big Easy" every year. Many of tourists visit the French Quarter (bottom) for its vibrant nightlife.

born in new orleans

When he was growing up, Percy Miller dreamed of doing great things. There was one problem with this dream. The little boy was living in the Calliope Projects, one of the worst slums in New Orleans. He had been born there on April 29, 1970. Most people in Calliope lived in poverty. Many were victims of violent crimes.

Percy's parents had divorced when he was five years old. His mother moved to California, but Percy and his brothers Kevin, Corey, and Vyshonn lived with their grandparents, Maxine and Claude Miller. Other kids also lived with the Millers. Sometimes, as many as twelve young people were living in their three-bedroom apartment. Miller often slept in the hall.

CALLIOPE PROJECT

In 1937 the United States was in the midst of the Great Depression. The U.S. Congress passed the Wagner Bill, which provided money to build low-cost housing.

New Orleans was the first city to receive funding from the Wagner Bill. Construction on the Calliope Project began in 1939. It opened in 1941 and consisted of 690 units. Rent for a one-bedroom apartment was just over eight dollars a month. An additional 860 units were added in 1954.

In 1981, the Calliope Project was officially renamed the B.W. Cooper Apartments to honor a longtime employee of the New Orleans Housing Authority. Despite this change, most residents still referred to it as the Calliope.

As industries moved out of New Orleans, so did whites. Eventually Calliope became almost entirely African American. The population density was more than 12,000 people per square mile, nearly six times the New Orleans average. Median household income was under $12,000, less than one-third the average for New Orleans—which in turn is considerably lower than the rest of the United States.

In 2005, Hurricane Katrina battered New Orleans. Flood waters up to six feet deep drenched the Calliope Project and forced residents to flee.

Calliope has produced other musical acts, including the Neville Brothers—a soul/R&B group—and teenage rapper Lil Chuckee.

Unlike many Calliope youngsters, Miller was lucky. His grandmother cared deeply for him and his younger siblings. She worked several jobs so that Miller could attend a private church school. She also told him that "the poorest person in the world is a person without a dream."

PUTTING DREAMS INTO PRACTICE

Doing great things was one of the dreams his grandmother inspired. He also had a more immediate dream: to help his family. Young Percy was a hard worker. When he was six, he began collecting aluminum to sell for recycling. Neighbors began tipping him to carry their groceries. He mowed lawns and ran errands to make extra money.

When he was about 16, Miller started a business selling cell phones. That helped put food on the family table. It also helped fuel his dream that some day, through hard work, he might be wealthy enough to buy everything his family needed.

Not everything Miller did during his teenage years in Calliope was on the up-and-up. He has admitted to doing some questionable, even criminal, things as a young man, including selling drugs. As he told Jay Babcock of the *Washington Post*,

> *"When you in the projects, you gotta do whatever it take to survive, to feed your family, because that's where your love at. . . . So you gotta do things, you gotta take penitentiary chances, and that's what I had to do. It's not something I wanted to do. I was on a mission, y'know. I wasn't hustlin' to buy a car or nothin' like that, I was hustlin' to survive. I was hustlin' to keep the bills paid, I was hustlin' so my brothers wouldn't have to hustle."*

Miller had one talent that few other hustlers in the Calliope Projects could match. He was a lights-out shooter with a basketball in his hands. He spent hours practicing his moves. Friends saw him shooing baskets even when the lights were out on the playground. Miller later said,

> "Basketball saved my life. When people were out doing bad things, they would see me and say, 'P, get to practice. Get from around here.' That's where my passion for basketball came from. That's where people respected me because I was so good. I was an All-American in high school and was always in the newspaper."

All his hard work and dedication paid off. As a high school player, he averaged more than 20 points a game and attracted the interest of several college coaches. The University of Houston offered him a *scholarship* to play point guard. Unfortunately he suffered a severe

Percy Miller hoped that his skill at basketball would help him to escape from the bad neighborhood where he lived.

knee injury before he could join the team. His hoop dreams were shattered.

Despite this disappointment, Miller persevered with his education. He attended Delgado Community College and then

enrolled at Southern University, where he took business classes.

LOVE AT FIRST SIGHT

During his high school days, Miller's basketball skills had attracted the attention of a young woman named Sonya. She was a cheerleader at a rival school in New Orleans. One evening they ran into each other at a party. "We ended up talking and exchanging telephone numbers," Miller later recalled. "She was just different from everyone else. She looked good. She had good conversation. That first day I was like, 'This girl is going to be mine.'"

His first impression was correct. As they continued to date, they found many things in common. They dreamed of getting out of the *ghetto* and becoming successful. Miller told said,

> *"We both refused to let the ghetto be a burden to us. We were just there for the time being, but we both dreamed of bigger things. In fact, she's probably a bigger dreamer than I am."*

Escaping ghetto life and achieving those "bigger things" can be very difficult. The Millers' dreams might have died in the Calliope Project. A family tragedy gave those dreams a chance to live.

Miller's grandfather went into a hospital for an operation. Because of *malpractice* by the doctors, the grandfather died. The hospital offered his grandmother a financial settlement. She accepted and gave Miller $10,000 from that settlement to help him start a new life. While it must have been difficult to leave his grandmother behind, Miller decided to move to the Richmond, California, area with Sonya to be near his mother. He also thought his family would be safer there. "I knew that eventually, if I didn't get my life or my act together, I'd probably go to jail or get killed," he later said.

AN IMPORTANT DECISION

Percy Miller had never before had $10,000, and he wasn't quite sure what to do with it. He and Sonya had to make a decision. Though they didn't know it at the time, that decision would have a profound influence on their lives—and on the hip-hop music industry as well.

Miller knew he wanted to start a business, but wasn't sure what to do at first. For a while, he and Sonya considered opening a car wash. But Miller decided that wasn't thinking big enough. Finally, they decided to open a record store in the San Francisco area. Sonya's parents had owned a record store back in New Orleans. She understood how the business operated.

"A car wash could have made a couple hundred thousand," Miller later told *Ebony* magazine. "But with a record company, there was no limit on the amount of money we could make." With that attitude, the name of the new store became obvious. It would be called No Limit Records. The store opened in 1988.

THE START OF SOMETHING BIG

The first months were *precarious*. At one point, the Millers lived in the back of the store to save money.

Aerial view of Richmond, California, which is part of the San Francisco Bay area. Certain areas of Richmond have very high rates of crime and violence. Percy Miller opened his record store in Richmond in 1988.

Eventually conditions improved. Miller applied the principles he had learned in his college business courses. Just as important, he paid careful attention to what his customers wanted. At that time, hip-hop on the West Coast was just beginning to change. A new style of music, known as **gangsta rap**, was becoming popular. This music had harsh, **explicit lyrics** about life on the streets, violence, and poverty.

Although this was the kind of music Miller's customers really wanted, at first larger record stores were reluctant to sell gangsta rap albums. Miller was not. He stocked albums by early gangsta rappers like N.W.A., Ice-T, Boogie Down Productions, and Kid Frost, as well as many lesser-known artists. Often, Miller would get new albums into his store the day they were released—long before his competitors.

THE INFLUENCE OF N.W.A.

Percy Miller's California record store profited by selling tapes and CDs produced by gangsta rappers. During the late 1980s and early 1990s, mainstream record companies generally considered the angry, profane lyrics of gangsta rap songs to be too extreme to sell in the large chain stores like Tower Records or Sam Goody's.

In 1988, a rap group from the area of Los Angeles known as Compton helped to bring gangsta rap into the mainstream. The group N.W.A. included rapper Ice Cube (pictured at right), Dr. Dre, Eazy-E, MC Ren, and DJ Yella. N.W.A.'s first album, *Straight Outta Compton*, included songs about guns, gang warfare, drugs, alcohol, and death. One track encouraged violence against police officers.

When people objected to the bad language and violence in the lyrics, the members of N.W.A. replied that they were rapping about the reality of urban life. Listeners agreed with them. The group's popularity increased even more when the FBI threatened their record distributor. The album went double platinum, selling about 2 million copies—many through small record stores like Miller's No Limit.

N.W.A. didn't stay together very long. Ice Cube left the group in 1990 and started a solo career. N.W.A. released an album without him in 1991. Dr. Dre left N.W.A. in 1992, and became an acclaimed music producer. His album *The Chronic*, released by Death Row Records in 1994, was another landmark album in hip-hop history. DJ Yella also became a noted music producer, while MC Ren released several successful solo albums. Eazy-E died in 1995.

In 2004 *Rolling Stone* magazine ranked N.W.A. number 83 on their list of the 100 greatest artists of all time. According to writer Ahmir Thompson, *Straight Outta Compton* is "the album that made hip-hop the new rock & roll. In the process, they changed the face of modern-day hip-hop."

Miller hoped to use the story to help his family prosper. He offered his brothers jobs at No Limit Records. His younger brother Kevin came to visit for a week, but didn't like California. Miller urged him to stay, but Kevin went back home. Soon afterward he was gunned down by a drug dealer. The loss affected Miller profoundly.

CHANGE OF DIRECTION

As he learned more about the type of music that young people wanted, Miller decided that he could create his own gangsta rap that was just as good as what other artists were making. He had a good singing voice. Some of his street experiences in New Orleans were the same that gangsta rappers used in their music. So he decided to start his own label. He would be the star.

Changing his company's direction was a big risk. Miller would have to work very hard to promote himself. Even then, there were no guarantees that he would be successful. Miller was willing to take the chance. He named his new label No Limit Records, after the name of his record store.

Of course, "Percy Miller" isn't exactly the kind of name that would sell a lot of records. Miller needed something different—something more flashy. He decided to call himself "Master P." Years later, he explained to *Jet* magazine that the nickname reflected his personality, because he "always ran things and took charge . . . always 100 percent in control, just like a master."

Two of his brothers, Corey and Vyshonn, helped Master P record some of his first songs. They also needed rap names. While growing up, Corey had witnessed violent crimes and other tough aspects of life in the ghetto. He came up with "see-murder," then changed the name to C-Murder. The "C" reflected the first initial of his name. Vyshonn called himself Silkk because, according to *Jet*, "he's extremely laid back, and he talks and raps very smooth, just like silk." He later revised the name to Silkk the Shocker.

Along with a couple of friends, the three brothers also formed a group called TRU (The Real Untouchables), which performed on a few tracks. TRU would eventually release several highly successful albums.

For the logo, or symbol, of his company, Master P chose an army tank. A tank is powerful and rolls over any obstacles. Master P thought of No Limit as an army and the people who worked with him as "No Limit soldiers." As he told Neil Strauss of the *New York Times*,

> *"If you do something to a soldier, they're going to turn and do it back to you. That's the way it is. And I'll fight. I would die for this: it's all I've got. If I don't have this, I'm going back to the ghetto. And I don't want to go back because I didn't want to be there in the first place."*

OFF TO A GOOD START

In 1991 No Limit Records released its first album, *Get Away Clean*. Master P rapped on more than half of the 13 tracks. TRU performed on several, and even his wife—calling herself Sonya C—lent her voice to one song. Writing several years later, Jason Birchmeier of allmusic.com wrote, "Though *Get Away Clean* doesn't boast impressive production values, or especially inventive rapping, for that matter, it does boast a lawless attitude very much influenced by N.W.A and the other early West Coast gangsta rap acts of the time."

Get Away Clean did well enough to encourage Master P to continue. The following year he released a second album, *Mama's Bad Boy*.

Master P spent a lot of time on the road, sometimes driving hundreds of miles and selling albums out of the back of his car. He often went into dangerous neighborhoods, assuring local gang members that he was only there to try to sell his music. Sometimes he gave an album to the driver of the car playing the loudest music.

He established several principles for promoting the label and its releases. One was bright, eye-catching covers. Another was including previews of upcoming releases in the booklet he inserted into every CD. As he explained to the *Washington Post*'s Jay Babcock,

> *"What I learned in the ghetto is that everybody wants more for their money. If you sell something for $20, they wanna know how can they get $25 worth. And that's what hustling is about: You gotta be able to give your customers more for their money, 'cause that's how you're going to keep them coming back to you."*

HEADING SOUTH

By 1994, his efforts began to pay off. That year, No Limit released *The Ghettos Tryin To Kill Me*. By this time, Master P had stopped imitating West Coast gangsta rap. Instead, No Limit's music began to draw on a style of New Orleans music known as **bounce**. Bounce's energetic rhymes were chanted in call-and-answer style. The performer would deliver a rhyme and invite the audience to respond with a one or two-line refrain. Audiences responded to bounce music's strong baseline and danceable beat.

The result was a different form of hip-hop music known as Southern hip-hop—sometimes just called "Dirty South." It was very energetic. Southern hip-hop songs often had a fast beat—sometimes 140 to 180 beats per minute. The songs were often written with a heavy bass sound, making them fun for dancing.

The *lyrics* of Southern hip-hop songs had fewer gang or drug references than the gangsta rap popular on the East and West coasts. Southern hip-hop songs were often about parties, fashion trends, and fancy cars. A few songs included lyrics about race relations and African-American life in the south.

The Ghettos Tryin To Kill Me also exhibited what would become one of the No Limit's *trademarks*: more tracks than its competitors. The album included 16 songs, some of which featured emerging rappers Big Ed, King George, JT the Bigga Figga, and San Quinn, as well as Silkk, C-Murder, Sonya C, and TRU. "There's no such thing as too much music," Master P explained.

Though Master P and No Limit Records weren't very well-known outside of California, *The Ghettos Tryin To Kill Me* sold well enough to make others in the record industry take notice. Master P didn't know it, but he would receive an offer that would make him a millionaire—if he accepted.

living up to its name

In 1994, the president of a major record company located in New York City called Master P. He offered him a recording contract worth a million dollars. At first, Master P was thrilled. Then he read the fine print. There was no money guaranteed beyond the first million. He couldn't work with any artists the record company didn't approve of. Above all, the company would own the rights to his rap name, the name No Limit Records, and all the music he produced. A light bulb went off in his head. "Basically, I would be selling my soul for a million dollars," he thought.

Master P faxed the contract to his attorney. The lawyer responded that it was a one-sided deal that favored the record company. On the other hand, he said, it probably was Master P's best opportunity to get rich quickly. Master P had two choices: take a million dollars now, or take a chance on even greater success in the future.

TURNING DOWN A MILLION DOLLARS

Master P decided not to sign the deal. In his book *Guaranteed Success*, the rapper says he was excited, not disappointed, to turn down the record company's million-dollar offer.

> *"Here I am, from the ghetto, and this president of the music company doesn't even know me. But he was willing to give me a million dollars for my talent. . . . And I started thinking, asking myself, How talented am I? If he's offering me a million dollars, what am I really worth?"*

He decided to find out. A few months later, a large company in California called Priority Records offered to act as No Limit's **distributor**, getting the company's releases into stores all over the country. They would pay him 85 percent of every sale. No Limit would have to pay the marketing costs for the albums. But Master P would still own his name and all the rights to his records.

Thanks to this deal, No Limit would move a million albums, in fact, within six months of signing the deal with Priority Records. These sales included many copies of Master P's fourth album, *99 Ways to Die*. Rather than the $1 million dollars the New York record company had offered, in that six-month period Master P earned more than $8 million.

FAST FACT

Priority Records was founded in Los Angeles in 1985. The company distributed releases by several of the most notable hip-hop labels. In addition to No Limit, they included Death Row Records, Roc-A-Fella Records, and Ruthless Records.

LAYING DOWN THE BEAT

Sales of No Limit's albums were boosted by another critical decision that Master P made around this time. Before 1994, Master P had been working with many different West Coast-based record producers to make No Limit's albums. In 1995, he began working with one production group, based in New Orleans, called Beats by the Pound. The group consisted of Craig "KLC" Lawson, Master P's cousin Raymond "Mo B. Dick" Poole, Craig "Craig B" Bazile, and Odell Vickers Jr.

It proved to be an ideal match. Over the next five years, Beats by the Pound would work almost exclusively with No Limit, helping to create the label's signature sound. As KLC later explained:

> "When I hooked up with P in 1995, he was still in Oakland. He was buying beats from like ten producers. When we came up, it just fit. I hooked him up with the beat for "Bout It, Bout It," and that turned out to be the biggest song on his first album."

That "first album" was *True*, the third album by TRU. It eventually was certified gold.

THE FIRST BIG SUCCESSES

The release of *Ice Cream Man* the following year represented a big step forward both for the label and for Master P. It was the first of his solo albums that Beats by the Pound produced, and it was also the first to be designated platinum for selling more than 1 million copies. "Master P took his music to a new level of quality on *Ice Cream Man*," said reviewer Jason Birchmeier. "Themes of drugs, violence, and ghetto life are **prevalent** and well exploited."

The album created such a buzz that Master P's next album, 1997's *Ghetto D*, sold more than 760,000 copies in the first week it was available.

Ghetto D included Master P's single "When I Say Uhhh," which became one of his signature songs. The song was eventually down-loaded more than a million times. The album eventually sold more than 3 million copies.

ADDING RAPPERS TO THE ROSTER

The No Limit team worked incredibly hard to make the label a suc-cess. In addition to turning out albums by Master P and TRU, the label also scored a hit for Vyshonn "Silkk" Miller, Master P's younger brother. Although it received little promotion, *The Shocker* became a major underground hit when it was released in 1996. The album was eventually certified platinum. Its success led Vyshonn to change his stage name to Silkk the Shocker.

In the mid-1990s, No Limit Records began signing many other tal-ented hip-hop performers. Many were associated with New Orleans. Master P and his No Limit soldiers worked to help make their records as successful as his own.

One of the first of these performers was a singer from New Orleans named Mia Young. Under the name Mia X, her first No Limit album, *Good Girl Gone Bad,* was released late in 1995. Two years later she released *Unlady Like,* which was certified gold and reached num-ber two on Billboard's R&B/Hip-Hot Album chart. Her third album *Mama Drama,* released in 1998, was nearly as successful. Many of No Limit's other artists accompanied Mia X on the songs she recorded for her albums.

Another performer, Richard "Fiend" Jones, had already released one album before signing with No Limit in 1997. Fiend appeared on Master P's *Ghetto D* and Mia X's *Unlady Like.* His first No Limit album,

No Limit recording artist Fiend (left) with KLC, a member of the label's famed production group Beats by the Pound. Fiend's two albums for No Limit, There's One in Every Family *(1998) and* Street Life *(1999) both went to number one on Billboard's hip-hop chart.*

There's One in Every Family, was released in 1998. It was certified gold and rose to the top of Billboard's R&B/Hip-Hop Albums chart. His second No Limit album, *Street Life*, also hit number one on the hip-hop albums chart, although it did not sell quite as well as *There's One in Every Family*.

Like Fiend, another rapper who joined No Limit in 1997 had previously released an album that had not sold well. McKinley "L'il Mac" Phipps changed his stage name to "Mac" when he joined No Limit. He was featured on several No Limit albums before his first solo effort for the label, *Shell Shocked*, was released in 1998. It was an immediate hit. Mac's second album, *World War III* (1999), was not quite as successful. In 2000, he joined the group 504 Boyz, a collective of other

═══ FAST FACT ═══

The name *504 Boyz* refers to telephone area code 504, which covers the New Orleans area. The group, which included many different No Limit performers at different times, released three albums between 2000 and 2005.

No Limit rappers such as Master P, Silkk the Shocker, and C-Murder. Mac was featured on the group's hit single "Wobble Wobble," and contributed to their first album, *Goodfellas* (2000).

Many people believe that after Master P himself, Michael "Mystikal" Tyler was No Limit's most important artist during the late 1990s. His album *Unpredictable* topped the R&B/hip-hop album chart in 1997 and was certified platinum. It included a hit single, "Ain't No Limit," which featured Silkk the Shocker. In 1998, Mystikal's *Ghetto Fabulous* reached number one on Billboard's Top R&B/Hip-Hop Albums chart and sold over a million copies.

Thanks to the successes of these artists, No Limit was definitely on the map. In September of 1997, No Limit Records had five of the top 150 albums in the country.

RETURNING TO HIS ROOTS

With No Limit Records's increasing emphasis on the New Orleans musical sound, it made sense for Master P to move back to the area with his family. So late in 1997 Master P bought a three-acre lakefront property in the Country Club of Louisiana. It is a very *upscale* housing development in Baton Rouge, Louisiana's capital city. The site included a house with 7,000 square feet, a garage for at least ten luxury cars, a recording studio, and a swimming pool. Master P paid the $1 million price in cash rather than taking out a mortgage. It marked a triumphant return for a man who had left the New Orleans area just seven years earlier with little else besides the $10,000 insurance payment that he had used to start his business.

As No Limit Records flourished, Master P began giving some of that money back to his community. He provided scholarships for students from Baton Rouge, donated $25,000 to the local Boy Scout organization, gave musical equipment to schools, and handed out Thanksgiving turkeys and winter coats. He also volunteered to speak to local students about the importance of staying in school and avoiding drugs and violence.

Things were good at No Limit Records, and they were about to get even better. Master P would soon add one of the biggest names in hip-hop to the label. In 1998, there was no question that No Limit was truly living up to its name.

By 1999, No Limit Records was one of the most successful hip-hop music labels. That year, Master P won an American Music Award for favorite Rap/Hip Hop artist.

Adding New Artists

During the 1990s, one of the biggest names in hip-hop was Snoop Dogg. Snoop's 1993 solo *debut*, *Doggystyle*, had entered the Billboard top 200 albums chart at number one, the first time a debut album had done so well. *Doggystyle* eventually sold more than 4 million copies. His second album, *Tha Doggfather*, was released in 1996 and surpassed 2 million in sales.

LOOKING FOR ANOTHER LABEL

The road to the top of the hip-hop world had not been easy or smooth for Snoop, whose real name is Calvin Broadus. He was born in 1971 in Long Beach, California. As a teenager, he was a member of the notorious Crips gang, and was arrested for possessing drugs.

His big break came when the noted gangsta rap music producer Dr. Dre invited Snoop to record several tracks on his album *The Chronic*. The album, which was released by Death Row Records in 1992, sold more than 8 million copies. Snoop was a large reason for the success, and fans clamored for him to record a solo album.

Dr. Dre produced *Doggystyle* but left Death Row shortly before Snoop's second album, *The Doggfather*, was released. Snoop didn't like working with Suge Knight, who operated Death Row. He decided to find another record company. In 1998, Snoop signed with No Limit. In his **autobiography**, *The Doggfather*, Snoop referred to Master P as "a stone-cold genius on the order of Dr. Dre" and added that:

> *"Working with No Limit has given me the kind of freedom I always looked for in making my music. Master P is on hand to give me guidance and suggestions, but there's no one looking over my shoulder trying to direct the flow one way or the other, and as a result, I can open it up and make room for both new sounds and old homies."*

Another reason for making the move was that Snoop's family originally came from the Deep South. Working in Baton Rouge felt like a homecoming. Snoop even bought a house in the same development as Master P. As Snoop explained, "There's something about the slowed-down and mellow pace of Southern life that soothes my soul like nowhere else. No Limit feels like home, and these days, home is where I most like to spend my time."

Snoop was by far the best-known rapper to join the No Limit label. As Joe Nick Potasio explained in *Spin* magazine, "It's the rap equivalent of an expansion football franchise buying a 35-year-old free agent with Super Bowl Rings on every finger." Record company executive Mark Shimmel added, "Snoop made a good move."

Snoop's first album with No Limit, *Da Game Is to Be Sold, Not to Be Told*, was released in August 1998. The album sold more than 500,000 copies in the first week after it was released, and became Snoop's third album to debut at number one on the Billboard charts. A number of No Limit artists sang with Snoop on the album, including Master P himself, Fiend, Mystikal, and Mia X.

Rap legend Snoop Dogg released three platinum-certified albums with No Limit Records between 1998 and 2000.

Da Game Is to Be Sold, Not to Be Told eventually sold more than 2 million copies. This helped No Limit's 1998 sales surpass two better-known record labels that specialized in hip-hop. Including Snoop's album, that year No Limit released four albums that went platinum, and three others that were certified gold. By comparison, Sean "P. Diddy" Combs's Bad Boy Records released just one gold album that year, while Death Row released none.

SEVERAL SUCCESSFUL ARTISTS

Snoop wasn't the only reason for No Limit's growing success. C-Murder met Awood "Magic" Johnson, a noted local rapper, at a party. Magic soon joined No Limit. His 1998 release *Sky's the Limit* reached number three on Billboard's hip-hop albums chart.

Master P's brothers were also active. In addition to performing on Snoop's *Da Game* album and releases by other No Limit artists, both released individual albums in 1998. Both Silkk the Shocker's *Charge It 2 da Game* and C-Murder's first album, *Life or Death*, went platinum and topped the R&B/hip-hop album charts that year.

Silkk the Shocker's 1999 album *Made Man* did even better. It sold more than 2 million copies and reached number one on both the Billboard top 200 albums chart and the R&B/hip-hop chart. *Made Man* included a number-one hit, "It Ain't My Fault 2," that featured his No Limit labelmate Mystikal. Another hit song from the album was called "Somebody Like Me."

> **FAST FACT**
>
> Silkk The Shocker was featured on Master P's 1998 hit single "Make 'Em Say Uhh!" That single would become one of Master P's most popular songs.

Master P. (right) attends a movie premiere with his brother, Vyshonn. Using the name Silkk the Shocker, Vyshonn recorded several hit albums for No Limit Records.

C-Murder released his second album, *Bossalinie*, in 1999, and his third album, *Trapped in Crime*, the next year. They did not do quite as well as his *Life or Death*, although both were certified gold and both hit number one on Billboard's R&B/Hip-Hop Albums chart.

By this time, No Limit Records was attracting significant attention from the national media. Highly respected national publications such as the *New York Times*, *Fortune* magazine, and the *Wall Street Journal* ran complimentary stories about the label.

MAKING HIS MARK IN MANY AREAS

One of the main reasons for this interest was that Master P had branched out in several other areas besides making records. He had a clothing line. A toy company created a Master P doll that yelled "Ya heard me?" He created No Limit Sports Management to negotiate contracts for several high-profile professional athletes.

Master P became especially successful in moviemaking. He started in 1997, when none of the major Hollywood studios was interested in a movie he wanted to make. The film was a raw examination of the New Orleans drug life called *I'm 'Bout It*. The story reflected Master P's own experiences while he was living there.

Master P decided to make the film himself. No Limit spent just $200,000 on the film. Master P directed and also starred in the movie,

> **FAST FACT**
>
> NFL running back Ricky Williams was the best-known client of No Limit Sports Management. Williams was the fifth player picked in the 1999 NFL draft. Other professional athletes that No Limit represented included NBA players Sam Cassell, Ron Mercer, Derek Anderson, Isaiah Rider, and Brian Shaw.

along with his friend Anthony "Boz" Boswell. They even worked the camera and lights. *I'm 'Bout It* looked rough and was never released in theaters, only on video. The cheap production values didn't matter to No Limit fans, however. The videos sold extremely well—in the first month, some 300,000 copies were sold, more than major studio hits like *Jerry Maguire*—and No Limit also profited from a soundtrack album. Once again Master P had proven that he didn't have to depend on established distribution channels.

Thanks to this success, No Limit's next film, a crime comedy called *I Got the Hook Up*, was released in theatres in 1998 by Dimension Films. The film, which cost $3.5 million to make, earned more than $10 million at the box office and another $10 million on video sales.

In the next few years, No Limit would make several more movies. Most were low-budget, direct-to-video films that were tied to albums by No Limit artists. These included *MP Da Last Don* (1998), which starred Master P, and *Da Game of Life*, starring Snoop Dogg. Master P would also act in several major films, including *Gone in 60 Seconds* (2000) with Nicolas Cage and Angelina Jolie, and *Hollywood Homicide* (2003) with Harrison Ford and Josh Hartnett.

HEADING INTO RETIREMENT

Master P was so busy with his other interests that he said he would retire from making records after releasing his seventh album, *MP Da Last Don,* in June of 1998. It was a double album with a staggering 29 tracks. It shot to the top of the Billboard 200 albums list with sales of more than 400,000 copies in the first week alone. *MP Da Last Don* would eventually become the best-selling album of Master P's career, with over 4 million copies sold.

Mystikal performs at the 2000 Billboard Music Awards in Las Vegas. The rapper was one of No Limit's biggest stars in the late 1990, releasing two hit albums and appearing on songs by many of the label's other stars.

Thanks to all these accomplishments, Master P had become one of the wealthiest people in the hip-hop world. In 1999 *Forbes* magazine ranked the rapper tenth on its list of the 40 highest paid American entertainers. The magazine estimated Master P's income at $56.5 million, and reported his net worth at more than $300 million.

For Master P, the money and fame was only one element of his success. Recognition of his talent from hip-hop fans and his peers was just as important. This came early in 1999, when Master P was named Favorite Rap/Hip-Hop Artist at the 26th annual American Music Awards ceremony.

Looking at all these accomplishments, it seemed that No Limit Records was becoming an irresistible force in the hip-hop world. "There ain't no goal to stop at," Master P told the *New York Times*. "I guess I want to be the ghetto Bill Gates." At the time Gates, the founder of Microsoft, was the wealthiest person in America.

Certainly, in 1999 there didn't seem to be any reason to doubt Snoop Dogg, who predicted, "If anyone is going to take hip-hop into the twenty-first century, it's going to be [Master P]." However, as the next few years would show, Snoop was wrong.

5

the decline of no limit

Despite the amazing success of No Limit, ominous signs for the future began to appear in 1999. In April of that year, Beats by the Pound ended its affiliation with the label. There were reports that the producers had left No Limit because Master P had refused to increase their pay. However, KLC had another explanation for the group's departure. He blamed basketball.

Master P had never lost his passion for the sport. He had even converted a tennis court at his home in Baton Rouge into a basketball court. In the summer of 1998, he scored more than 20 points in a charity game against players from the National Basketball Association

(NBA). That performance made Master P wonder how good he could really be if he truly focused all his energy on the sport.

HOOPING IT UP

During the summer of 1998, under the name Percy Miller, he tried out for the Fort Wayne Fury of the minor-league Continental Basketball Association (CBA). Miller played well enough to be offered a contract by the team. He decided to play the 1998-99 season for Fort Wayne, with an eye toward bigger things in the future. Miller explained his thinking to J.R. Ross of the *Chicago Sun-Times*:

> *"I want to be here and show people I'm serious about this and build my talent and then go to the NBA. I'm growing. I'm growing and getting better."*

He certainly wasn't in it for the money. The Fury paid him $1,000 a month salary and $15 a day for meals. Also, his music success didn't mean anything on the basketball court. Fury coach Keith Smart said:

> *"He's not Master P here; he's Percy Miller. When you're Percy Miller, you can learn because you know you haven't done anything."*

During that season in the CBA, Miller learned enough to be invited to training camp by an NBA team, the Charlotte Hornets, in 1999. Miller lasted in camp for several weeks before being cut. Later that fall, he tried out for another NBA team, the Toronto Raptors. Again, however, he didn't make the squad.

MINOR LEAGUE BASKETBALL

The Continental Basketball Association (CBA) was established on April 23, 1946. That was about six weeks before the better-known National Basketball Association (NBA) was founded.

While the NBA had teams in major American cities, the CBA began with six small cities in Pennsylvania. (Originally the league was called the Eastern Pennsylvania Basketball League.) Teams came and went almost every year. At various points during its history teams from 40 states, the District of Columbia, Puerto Rico, Canada, and Mexico took part.

Fort Wayne, where Percy Miller played during the 1998-99 season, was typical. The city had been the original home of the NBA's Pistons, until that franchise moved to Detroit in 1957. The CBA's Fort Wayne Fury was formed in 1992. The team disbanded in 2001, when the league shut down briefly because of financial trouble.

CBA players didn't make much money. When Percy Miller was playing in the late 1990s, the highest salary was only about $40,000 a season. Even benchwarmers on NBA teams make millions of dollars.

The appeal of playing in the CBA was that for some players, it could be a path to the NBA. In the 1980s and 1990s, players like Tim Legler and Mario Elie went from the CBA to the NBA. Percy Miller hoped to follow this same path.

In 2001, the CBA declared bankruptcy. Its name and assets were purchased by another minor basketball league, the International Basketball Association (IBA). The new league, which included some former CBA teams, operated under the Continental Basketball Association name beginning in the 2001-02 season. The league closed down for good after the 2008-09 season.

Today, many young players who hope to eventually play in the National Basketball Association compete in the 16-team NBA Development League.

Being cut twice by NBA teams didn't end Percy Miller's hoop dreams. In 2001-02 he played 13 games for the San Diego Stingrays and in 2004-05 he spent some time with the Las Vegas Rattlers.

Miller's focus on basketball angered some No Limit artists, who felt that he was not involved enough in the label's business. Beats by the Pound's KLC explained:

> *"It wasn't the money that made us leave. It was the communication. When [Master P] decided to go pursue his basketball career, it [messed] up our communication. Whenever we had to talk to him, we had to go through somebody. When it goes through somebody, it gets back to him all [messed] up."*

Master P simply hired other producers. He also continued to release records, even while playing basketball. In 1999, while working out for the Raptors, the rapper released *Only God Can Judge Me*. It went to the top of Billboard's R&B/hip-hop chart. His ninth album, *Ghetto Postage*, was released the following year. It reached number two on the R&B/hip-hop chart.

ARTISTS LEAVING THE LABEL

Beats by the Pound were among the first to leave No Limit Records, but they would not be the last. Mystikal also left the label in 1999. He signed with Jive Records, which had released one of his earlier albums, and released the album *Let's Get Ready* in 2000. In his review, Jason Birchmeier said that Mystikal had been "No Limit's most impressive rapper" and commented:

> *The album [Let's Get Ready] benefits from the production and songwriting variety that No Limit was never able to accomplish."*

In 2000, Fiend left No Limit to start his own record label, Fiend Entertainment. That same year, after the release of his third No Limit album, *Tha Last Meal*, Snoop Dogg also left the label. At the time, Snoop reportedly felt that he was not earning enough from his albums. By leaving he was able to gain more control over his career. Like Fiend, Snoop started his own label, Doggystyle Records. He made a deal with a major record company, MCA, that offered Snoop better marketing, promotional and distribution opportunities than No Limit could provide. Yet in 2010, Snoop looked back favorably on his time with No Limit, commenting:

> *"[Tha Last Meal] gave me a chance to really sprout out and become who I was, put a record together the way I felt, and work with the people I wanted to work with. Master P and I made great music together, and this record right here put me in a strong position. This record had heat on it, man."*

PROBLEMS WITH THE LAW

In 2001, Mac left the label for a very different reason. He was sentenced to 30 years in prison for his involvement in the shooting death of a young man in a nightclub.

Mac wasn't the only No Limit soldier with legal problems. In 2002, C-Murder was involved in the shooting of a fan. He was eventually convicted of second-degree murder and sentenced to life imprisonment.

By 2002 No Limit's roster of artists had essentially shrunk to Master P himself, his brothers Silkk the Shocker and C-Murder, Mia X, and Magic. Magic departed in 2003 after the release of his third album, *White Eyes*. The album had not sold very well, and Magic was very angry. Mia X soon got out of the music business altogether, and didn't release any more albums for No Limit or any other label.

Corey "C-Murder" Miller (left) with hip-hop performer Neyo.
Master P's brother is currently serving a life sentence in prison
after being convicted of murder in 2003.

Many people began to consider No Limit as little more than a label for the Miller family. This belief was heightened when P's son, now known as L'il Romeo and just 11 years old, released his first album, *L'il Romeo*. It was quickly certified gold and the single "My Baby" reached number one on Billboard's Hot R&B/Hip-Hop songs.

BACK TO THE WEST COAST

Master P had become increasingly unhappy in Baton Rouge. He had to sell an unfinished recording studio in Baton Rouge to meet construction bills. He also thought he was being discriminated against, even though he contributed hundreds of thousands of dollars to charity. In 2002 he moved to Beverly Hills, California. He said he felt safer and more comfortable there.

> === FAST FACT ===
> In 2002, as Master P left the New Orleans area, the Charlotte Hornets—the first NBA team he had tried out for—moved to the city. The team is currently known as the New Orleans Hornets.

He tried to boost the No Limit label by adding lesser-known artists. One was Darwin "Choppa" Turner, who released two albums, *Choppa Style* (2002) and *Straight from the N.O.* (2003). Neither one did well. Another was Shante "Curren$y" Franklin who signed with No Limit in 2003. Curren$y recorded songs with the 504 Boyz and with Master P. However, No Limit never released an album of Curren$y's solo material, and he left the label in 2004. Curren$y later said that while with No Limit, he often felt that Master P had been too busy to spend time with him.

These moves didn't seem to help. Late in 2003, No Limit Records quietly announced that it was *bankrupt*.

From Master P to P. Miller

The No Limit label was gone, but under bankruptcy laws, Master P was able to keep much of the money he had made. He quickly began a new label, called the New No Limit. The following year, he established Guttar Music Entertainment to distributed his releases. However, over the next decade his companies would release only a handful of records.

The first was Master P's *Good Side, Bad Side*, released in March, 2004. The album proved that he still had a lot of fans, rising to number 3 on the R&B/hip-hop list and number 11 on the top 200.

Silkk the Shocker released *Based on a True Story* for the new label in the fall of 2004. However, it did not sell anywhere near as well as Silkk's previous four albums had.

Two more of Master P's albums came out in 2005. They were *Ghetto Bill* and *Living Legend: Certified D-Boy*. Neither one did particularly well in sales. Critics didn't think much of them either. Steve Juon of RapReviews.com said of *Ghetto Bill*, "Master P may be hitting a creative dry spell." David Jeffries of allmusic.com called *Living Legend* "a confusing sidestep . . . only hardcore fans need be excited."

FINDING A PURPOSE

In September, 2005, Hurricane Katrina devastated New Orleans. For Master P, the storm served as a wakeup call. He later said:

> *"I discovered my life's true purpose after Hurricane Katrina. I knew that no matter what I was going through in my own life, I had to figure out how to be there for other people—my family, my friends, and the many others who lost everything due to the hurricane. . . . One of my goals that relates to my ultimate purpose is to help rebuild our communities."*

Realizing this goal actually took two forms. One was practical. Miller continued his involvement with charities, creating some new ones and lending his name and financial support to others. One of his first acts after Katrina was donating profits from *Living Legend* to relief of the survivors.

He also established basketball programs with retired superstar Magic Johnson, set up foundations for at-risk youth and for feeding the homeless, and replaced former president Bill Clinton as the keynote speaker at an NAACP convention.

CLEANING UP THE LYRICS

The other form was more spiritual and moral in nature. One day he watched Oprah Winfrey interviewing noted African-American

A flooded New Orleans neighborhood in the aftermath of Hurricane Katrina, 2005. Master P was angry and upset about the effect of the storm on his community, and he worked to raise money to help those who were most affected by the disaster.

spokesman Al Sharpton on her television show. They were discussing the negative influence of lyrics in hip-hop music. Master P became very uncomfortable. As he explained to Essence.com,

> *"To be honest my conscience was like, P, it's people like you that's part of the problem. We're giving these kids the wrong information. I can do something about this; I can really take a stand and do something about this. If I'm in the car with my kids and my wife and have to turn my own music down when it comes on, that's a problem. I need to get my act together. So it made me like 'P, you have to do something. Oprah's talking to you.'"*

He chose to do something. Along with Romeo, he founded Take a Stand Records in 2007. He said it would be the only hip-hop label committed to what he called "responsible" lyrics with positive messages. He and Romeo made hip-hop history with the release of the label's first record, *Miller Boyz: Hip Hop History*. It was the first time a father and son had worked together to produce an entire album.

The same year, he published *Guaranteed Success*, a book based on his own experiences in creating wealth.

Master P worked with NBA superstar Earvin "Magic" Johnson to establish basketball programs for underprivileged children.

Donald Trump, former basketball star Magic Johnson, and Robert Kiyosaki—author of the best-selling book *Rich Dad, Poor Dad*—joined him on a tour to promote the book and encourage people to believe that they could improve themselves financially.

ANOTHER NAME CHANGE

In the summer of 2008, the name "Master P" went into retirement. It was replaced by the name "P. Miller" in another change of identity. At the time, the entrepreneur said:

"I'm changing my name because Master P is who I used to be. I call it my childhood, and P. Miller marks my manhood. There's a lot of people out there who are afraid to grow up and change, but I'm not and P. Miller is the evolution of me, Percy Miller, the entrepreneur, the businessman."

INSPIRATIONAL AUTHOR

Percy Miller has said that one of his goals is to help people become successful. He included many of the financial and spiritual lessons he has learned during his career into his 2007 book *Guaranteed Success: When You Never Give Up.* He uses several examples from his own life to illustrate powerful lessons he learned.

The book is very positive and upbeat. Much of it consists of questions he asks readers to answer and write down in the spaces provided.

He believes seeing goals and aspirations written in black and white, instead of just thinking about them, makes them easier to achieve.

In the book, he emphasizes seven factors that keep people from being successful. These include fear, procrastination, past failures and successes, wasting time, comfort, negative attitudes, and environment. He believes all of these factors are under an individual's control, and can therefore be overcome with hard work and dedication.

Miller didn't waste any time emphasizing his new identity. He worked with Wal-Mart to promote his line of affordable clothing, P. Miller Designs.

With all these changes going on, one thing remained the

same. This was his love for basketball. He made one final try at the NBA in 2005, playing in a summer league with a team sponsored by the Sacramento Kings. Three years later, he showed he could still compete. He played in the NBA McDonalds All-Star Celebrity Game. Miller scored 17 points and sank the game-winning free throws to help his team win by a single point.

For a while, it appeared that Romeo might fulfill his father's basketball legacy. After starring for his high school basketball team, he received a scholarship to play for the University of Southern California. Romeo was a member of the team for two years, although he didn't see much playing time. After that, he decided to devote full time to his studies to better prepare for his career as a music industry executive.

P. Miller continued his own efforts to improve the communities around him. In 2010, he pledged to build a school in Haiti after the country's devastating earthquake. He also announced the formation of Better Black Television. That

Romeo Miller poses with a young fan at the 2011 Nickelodeon Kids Choice Awards ceremony. Romeo has made his mark as both a rapper and an actor. In January 2011 he announced the formation of a new record label called No Limit Forever.

P. Miller arrives at the 2011 BET Awards with former Destiny's Child singer Kelly Rowland. The hip-hop entrepreneur remains active by helping his son build No Limit Forever Records and working with rapper Gucci Mane on an upcoming film.

was a new cable network that would provide positive messages for its viewers.

LEAVING A GOOD NAME

It's not certain what the upcoming years will bring for P. Miller. But it appears that leaving a legacy will be one of his primary motivations. He once told a reporter,

> *"I want to have a name powerful enough to pass down. I want people to say about my great-great-grandchildren 200 years from now, 'Oh, those are the Millers. They are good people.' More than a car, more than a house, more than a business, to me, a good name is the most important thing I could leave behind."*

And just as he did two decades ago when he was almost penniless and didn't have much except a dream of being successful, P. Miller puts no limit on achieving that goal of leaving behind a good name.

Chronology

1969 Percy Miller is born on April 29 in New Orleans, Louisiana.

1989 Miller's son, Percy Romeo Miller Jr., is born on August 19 in New Orleans.

1990 Miller and his family move to Richmond, California after receiving a $10,000 malpractice check and open No Limit record store.

1991 Now known as Master P, he releases *Get Away Clean*, his first album for the No Limit label.

1995 Master P and No Limit Records sign a favorable distribution deal with Priority Records.

1996 No Limit releases the hit albums *Ice Cream Man* (Master P) and *The Shocker* (Silkk).

1997 Master P's *Ghetto D* is released. It contains his song "Make 'Em Say Uhh!" and becomes his best-selling album; the Miller family moves to Baton Rouge, Louisiana, and buys a home in an exclusive community; the direct-to-video movie *I'm 'Bout It* becomes a surprise hit.

1998 Snoop Dogg releases *Da Game Is to Be Sold, Not to Be Told*, his first album for No Limit; the label sells 28 million copies of its records, more than any other hip-hop label that year.

1999 Silkk the Shocker's *Made Man* sells more than 2 million copies; Master P receives the American Music Award for Favorite Rap/Hip-Hop Artist; Beats by the Pound ends its association with No Limit Records; Percy Miller tries out unsuccessfully for two NBA teams; Mystikal leaves the label.

Chronology

2000 No Limit stars continue to leave the label, among them Fiend and Snoop Dogg.

2001 No Limit rapper Mac is sentenced to prison for 30 years because of his involvement with a murder.

2002 C-Murder is involved in a killing for which he will eventually be sentenced to life imprisonment; Master P and his family move to Beverly Hills.

2003 No Limit Records files for bankruptcy.

2004 Master P launches New No Limit Records.

2005 Guttar Music Entertainment is established by Master P and Romeo to distribute New No Limit releases.

2007 Master P starts Take a Stand Records; publishes *Guaranteed Success: When You Never Give Up.*

2008 Master P announces that he will now be known as P. Miller.

2010 P. Miller launches the Better Black Television network.

2011 Romeo Miller launches No Limit Forever Records; P. Miller works with rapper Gucci Mane on a film project.

Glossary

autobiography—the story of a person's life that the person writes himself or herself.

bankrupt—a legal condition that occurs when a business does not have enough money to pay bills or function.

bounce—a style of rap music with roots in New Orleans that is based on the "drag rap" beat.

debut—first appearance of something, such as an album.

distributor—a company that works with a record label to get music albums into retail stores and outlets where they can be sold.

entrepreneur—owner or manager of a business enterprise who makes money through risk and hard work.

explicit lyrics—song lyrics that include profanity and graphic references to sex, drugs, violence, racism, and other themes.

gangsta rap—a style of rap music that emphasizes violence, drug use, and hostility toward women and authority as it describes inner-city life.

ghetto—a slum, often used to describe a area where poor members of a minority group live.

lyrics—words to a song.

malpractice—medical error that can result in serious injury or death.

Glossary

precarious—uncertain; having a high chance of failing.

prevalent—particularly common.

record label—a company that produces, promotes, and distributes recordings for its artists.

scholarship—financial assistance that enables a student to attend a college or university.

trademarks—well-known characteristics or features of a person or organization.

upscale—reflecting a high degree of wealth.

Further Reading

Cameron, Andrea. *The 10 Most Influential Hip-Hop Artists*. New York: Franklin Watts, 2008.

Carlson-Berne, Emma. *Snoop Dogg*. Philadelphia: Mason Crest, 2007.

Deutsch, Stacia, and Rhody Cohon. *Jermaine Dupri*. Philadelphia: Mason Crest, 2009.

Gaines, Ann Graham, and Reggie Majors. *The Hip-Hop Scene*. Berkeley Heights, N.J.: Enslow Publishers, 2010.

Kenney, Karen Latchana. *Cool Hip-Hop Music: Create & Appreciate What Makes Music Great!* Edina, Minn.: Abdo Publishing, 2008.

Miller, Percy. *Guaranteed Success: When You Never Give Up*. West Babylon, N.Y.: Urban Books, 2007.

Torres, John. *Timbaland*. Hockessin, Delaware: Mitchell Lane, 2008.

Zafori, Wendy Garofoli. *Hip-Hop History*. Mankato, Minn.: Capstone Books, 2010.

Internet Resources

http://www.takeastandrecords.com

The official website of Take a Stand records, with news, videos, scholarship information and other items of interest.

http://www.bbtv.com

Official website of Percy Miller's Better Black Television, including program descriptions, schedule information, music videos, and merchandise.

http://www.trutanksoldiers.com

Billed as the longest-running No Limit site, Tru Tank Soldiers has photos, videos, news, coverage of VH1 honors, and other links.

http://www.pmilleronline.com/home

P. Miller's personal website, with news, bio, pictures, videos, and store.

http://www.officialromeo.com

Official website for Romeo Miller, with bio, photos, message board, news, and more.

index

Entries in **bold italic** refer to captions

JIM WHITING has written more than 100 children's non-fiction books and edited well over 150 more during an especially diverse writing career. He published *Northwest Runner* magazine for more than 17 years. His other credits include advising a national award-winning high school newspaper, sports editor for the *Bainbridge Island Review*, event and venue writeups and photography for America Online, articles in dozens of magazines, light verse in the *Saturday Evening Post*, the first piece of original fiction to appear in *Runner's World*, and official photographer for the Antarctica Marathon. For more information, visit www.jimwhiting.com.